Dips & Spreads

D0368850

Starters that make entertaining a snap

cheesy pizza dip

PREP: 10 min. | TOTAL: 15 min. | MAKES: 2½ cups or 20 servings, 2 Tbsp. each.

▶ what you need!

1 lb. (16 oz.) VELVEETA Pasteurized Prepared Cheese Product, cut into ½-inch cubes

1 tomato, chopped

1½ oz. pepperoni, chopped

▶ make it!

COMBINE ingredients in 1½-qt. microwaveable bowl.

MICROWAVE on HIGH 4 to 5 min. or until VELVEETA is completely melted, stirring every 2 min.

SERVE hot with breadsticks or assorted cut-up fresh vegetables.

CREATIVE LEFTOVERS:
Cover and refrigerate any leftover dip. Reheat and drizzle over hot baked potatoes or cooked pasta for an easy cheesy sauce.

VELVEETA
hot 'n cheesy crab dip

PREP: 5 min. | TOTAL: 10 min. | MAKES: 2½ cups or 20 servings, 2 Tbsp. each.

▶ what you need!

1 lb. (16 oz.) VELVEETA Pasteurized Prepared Cheese Product, cut into ½-inch cubes

1 can (6½ oz.) crabmeat, drained, flaked

4 green onions, sliced

½ cup chopped red bell peppers

½ cup BREAKSTONE'S or KNUDSEN Sour Cream

⅛ tsp. ground red pepper (cayenne)

▶ make it!

MIX first 4 ingredients in large microwaveable bowl. Microwave on HIGH 5 min. or until VELVEETA is completely melted, stirring after 3 min.

STIR in remaining ingredients.

SERVE with WHEAT THINS Original Snacks or assorted cut-up fresh vegetables.

KEEPING IT SAFE:
Hot dips should be discarded after sitting at room temperature for 2 hours or longer.

JAZZ IT UP:
Top with additional BREAKSTONE'S or KNUDSEN Sour Cream before serving.

garden vegetable dip

PREP: 10 min. | TOTAL: 3 hours 10 min. | MAKES: 20 servings, 2 Tbsp. each.

▶ what you need!

2 pkg. (8 oz. each) PHILADELPHIA Cream Cheese, softened

½ cup KRAFT Blue Cheese Dressing

½ cup finely chopped broccoli

1 medium carrot, shredded

▶ make it!

MIX cream cheese and dressing until well blended. Stir in vegetables; cover.

REFRIGERATE several hours or until chilled.

SERVE with assorted NABISCO Crackers.

BEST OF SEASON:
Take advantage of the fresh seasonal vegetables that are available. Cut up zucchini, carrots, cucumbers and bell peppers to serve as dippers with this creamy dip.

VARIATION:
Prepare as directed, using PHILADELPHIA Neufchâtel Cheese and KRAFT Light Blue Cheese Reduced Fat Dressing.

hot broccoli dip

PREP: 30 min. | TOTAL: 30 min. | MAKES: 2½ cups or 20 servings, 2 Tbsp. each.

▶ what you need!

1 loaf (1½ lb.) round sourdough bread

½ cup chopped celery

½ cup chopped red bell peppers

¼ cup chopped onions

2 Tbsp. butter or margarine

1 lb. (16 oz.) VELVEETA Pasteurized Prepared Cheese Product, cut into ½-inch cubes

1 pkg. (10 oz.) frozen chopped broccoli, thawed, drained

¼ tsp. dried rosemary leaves, crushed

Few drops hot pepper sauce

▶ make it!

HEAT oven to 350°F.

CUT slice from top of bread loaf; remove center, leaving 1-inch-thick shell. Cut removed bread into bite-sized pieces. Cover shell with top of bread; place on baking sheet with bread pieces. Bake 15 min. Cool slightly.

MEANWHILE, cook and stir celery, bell peppers and onions in butter in medium saucepan on medium heat until tender. Reduce heat to low. Add VELVEETA; cook until melted, stirring frequently. Add broccoli, rosemary and hot pepper sauce; mix well. Cook until heated through, stirring constantly.

SPOON into bread loaf. Serve hot with toasted bread pieces, NABISCO Crackers and/or assorted cut-up fresh vegetables.

USE YOUR MICROWAVE:
Mix celery, bell peppers, onions and butter in 2-qt. microwaveable bowl. Microwave on HIGH 1 min. Add VELVEETA, broccoli, rosemary and hot pepper sauce; mix well. Microwave 5 to 6 min. more or until VELVEETA is melted, stirring after 3 min.

VARIATION:
Omit bread loaf. Spoon dip into serving bowl. Serve with crackers and assorted cut-up fresh vegetables as directed.

SUBSTITUTE:
Prepare as directed, using VELVEETA Made With 2% Milk Reduced Fat Pasteurized Prepared Cheese Product.

last-minute cheesy hot dip

PREP: 10 min. | TOTAL: 25 min. | MAKES: 2½ cups dip or 20 servings, 2 Tbsp. dip and 4 crackers each.

▶ what you need!

1 pkg. (8 oz.) PHILADELPHIA Cream Cheese, softened

1½ cups KRAFT Shredded Colby & Monterey Jack Cheese

5 green onions, thinly sliced

⅓ cup KRAFT Real Mayo Mayonnaise

1 Tbsp. GREY POUPON Harvest Coarse Ground Mustard

2 Tbsp. chopped PLANTERS Smoked Almonds

RITZ Simply Socials Golden Wheat Crackers

▶ make it!

HEAT oven to 350°F.

MIX cheeses, onions, mayo and mustard in 9-inch pie plate; top with nuts.

BAKE 15 min. Serve with crackers.

VELVEETA cheesy bean dip

PREP: 5 min. | TOTAL: 11 min. | MAKES: 3¼ cups or 26 servings, 2 Tbsp. each.

▶ what you need!

1 lb. (16 oz.) Mild Mexican VELVEETA Pasteurized Prepared Cheese Product with Jalapeño Peppers, cut into ½-inch cubes

1 can (16 oz.) TACO BELL HOME ORIGINALS Refried Beans*

½ cup TACO BELL HOME ORIGINALS Thick 'N Chunky Salsa

▶ make it!

MIX all ingredients in microwaveable bowl.

MICROWAVE on HIGH 5 to 6 min. or until VELVEETA is completely melted and mixture is well blended, stirring after 3 min.

SERVE with tortilla chips or assorted cut-up fresh vegetables.

USE YOUR STOVE:
Mix all ingredients in medium saucepan. Cook on medium-low heat until VELVEETA is completely melted and mixture is well blended, stirring frequently. Serve as directed.

BEAN DIP OLÉ:
Prepare as directed, omitting the salsa, using VELVEETA Pasteurized Prepared Cheese Product and adding 1 undrained 4-oz. can chopped green chilies.

SPECIAL EXTRA:
To serve in a bread bowl, cut a lengthwise slice from the top of 1-lb. round bread loaf. Remove center of loaf, leaving 1-inch-thick shell. Cut removed bread into bite-sized pieces to serve with dip. Fill bread bowl with hot dip just before serving.

*TACO BELL and HOME ORIGINALS are registered trademarks owned and licensed by Taco Bell Corp.

VELVEETA chili dip

PREP: 5 min. | TOTAL: 10 min. | MAKES: 3 cups or 24 servings, 2 Tbsp. each.

▶ what you need!

1 lb. (16 oz.) VELVEETA Pasteurized Prepared Cheese Product, cut into ½-inch cubes

1 can (15 oz.) chili with or without beans

▶ make it!

MIX VELVEETA and chili in microwaveable bowl.

MICROWAVE on HIGH 5 min. or until VELVEETA is completely melted and mixture is well blended, stirring after 3 min.

SERVE hot with tortilla chips, RITZ Toasted Chips or assorted cut-up fresh vegetables.

TO HALVE:
Mix ½ lb. (8 oz.) VELVEETA Pasteurized Prepared Cheese Product, cut up, and ¾ cup canned chili in 1-qt. microwaveable bowl. Microwave on HIGH 3 to 4 min. or until VELVEETA is melted, stirring after 2 min. Serve as directed. Makes 1¼ cups or 10 servings, 2 Tbsp. each.

VELVEETA chipotle dip

PREP: 10 min. | TOTAL: 16 min. | MAKES: 3¼ cups or 26 servings, 2 Tbsp. each.

▶ what you need!

- 1 lb. (16 oz.) VELVEETA Pasteurized Prepared Cheese Product, cut into ½-inch cubes

- 2 Tbsp. chipotle peppers in adobo sauce, chopped

- 1 container (16 oz.) BREAKSTONE'S or KNUDSEN Sour Cream

▶ make it!

MIX VELVEETA and peppers in microwaveable bowl.

MICROWAVE on HIGH 4 to 6 min. or until VELVEETA is melted, stirring after 3 min. Stir in sour cream.

SERVE with assorted cut-up fresh vegetable dippers.

SIZE-WISE:
Savor every bite of this tasty, hot dip. Each 2 Tbsp. serving goes a long way on flavor.

TO HALVE:
Prepare as directed, cutting all ingredients in half. Makes about 1½ cups or 13 servings, about 2 Tbsp. each.

VELVEETA ranch dip

PREP: 5 min. | TOTAL: 11 min. | MAKES: 3¼ cups or 26 servings, 2 Tbsp. each.

▶ what you need!

1 lb. (16 oz.) VELVEETA Pasteurized Prepared Cheese Product, cut into ½-inch cubes

1 container (8 oz.) BREAKSTONE'S or KNUDSEN Sour Cream

1 cup KRAFT Ranch Dressing

▶ make it!

MIX all ingredients in microwaveable bowl.

MICROWAVE on HIGH 6 min. or until VELVEETA is completely melted and mixture is well blended, stirring every 2 min.

SERVE with assorted cut-up fresh vegetables or your favorite NABISCO Crackers.

VELVEETA PEPPER JACK RANCH DIP:
Prepare as directed, using VELVEETA Pepper Jack Pasteurized Prepared Cheese Product.

HOW TO SERVE IT COLD:
This versatile dip can also be served cold. Just prepare as directed; cool completely. Cover and refrigerate several hours or until chilled. Serve as directed.

VELVEETA
southwestern corn dip

PREP: 5 min. | TOTAL: 10 min. | MAKES: 3½ cups or 28 servings, 2 Tbsp. each.

▶ what you need!

1 lb. (16 oz.) VELVEETA Pasteurized Prepared Cheese Product, cut into ½-inch cubes

1 can (11 oz.) corn with red and green bell peppers, drained

3 jalapeño peppers, seeded, minced

1 red onion, finely chopped

½ cup fresh cilantro, finely chopped

½ cup BREAKSTONE'S or KNUDSEN Sour Cream

▶ make it!

MIX VELVEETA and corn in large microwaveable bowl.

MICROWAVE on HIGH 5 min. or until VELVEETA is completely melted, stirring after 3 min. Stir in remaining ingredients.

SERVE with WHEAT THINS Original Snacks or assorted cut-up fresh vegetables.

TO HALVE:
Mix ingredients as directed in 1-qt. microwaveable bowl, cutting all ingredients in half. Microwave on HIGH 3 to 4 min. or until VELVEETA is completely melted, stirring after 2 min. Serve as directed. Makes 1½ cups or 12 servings, 2 Tbsp. each.

KEEPING IT SAFE:
Hot dips should be discarded after sitting at room temperature for 2 hours or longer.

VELVEETA ultimate queso dip

PREP: 5 min. | TOTAL: 10 min. | MAKES: 3 cups or 24 servings, 2 Tbsp. each.

▶ what you need!

1 lb. (16 oz.) VELVEETA Pasteurized Prepared Cheese Product, cut into ½-inch cubes

1 can (10 oz.) RO*TEL Diced Tomatoes & Green Chilies, undrained

▶ make it!

MIX ingredients in microwaveable bowl.

MICROWAVE on HIGH 5 min. or until VELVEETA is completely melted, stirring after 3 min.

SERVE with assorted cut-up vegetables, WHEAT THINS Original Snacks or tortilla chips.

SIZE-WISE:
When eating appetizers at social occasions, preview your choices and decide which you'd like to try instead of taking some of each.

CREATIVE LEFTOVERS:
Refrigerate any leftover dip. Reheat and serve spooned over hot baked potatoes or cooked pasta.

SUBSTITUTE:
Prepare using Mild Mexican VELVEETA Pasteurized Prepared Cheese Product.

*RO*TEL is a registered trademark of ConAgra Foods, Inc.*

creamy coconut dip

PREP: 5 min. | TOTAL: 3 hours 5 min. | MAKES: 48 servings, 2 Tbsp. each.

▶ what you need!

1 pkg. (8 oz.) PHILADELPHIA Cream Cheese, softened

1 can (15 oz.) cream of coconut

1 tub (16 oz.) COOL WHIP Whipped Topping, thawed

▶ make it!

BEAT cream cheese and cream of coconut in large bowl with wire whisk until well blended.

ADD COOL WHIP; gently stir until well blended. Cover. Refrigerate several hours or until chilled.

SERVE with HONEY MAID Grahams Honey Sticks, HONEY MAID Honey Grahams or cut-up fresh fruit.

JAZZ IT UP:
Garnish with toasted BAKER'S ANGEL FLAKE Coconut just before serving.

2-minute delicious PHILLY dip

PREP: 5 min. | TOTAL: 5 min. | MAKES: ½ cup dip or 4 servings, 2 Tbsp. dip and 3 crackers each.

▶ what you need!

¼ cup PHILADELPHIA Cream Cheese Spread

1 Tbsp. KRAFT CATALINA Dressing

2 Tbsp. sliced black olives

TRISCUIT Thin Crisps

▶ make it!

MIX first 3 ingredients until well blended.

SERVE with crackers.

VARIATION:
Serve with celery sticks instead of/in addition to the crackers.

SUBSTITUTE:
Prepare using green olives.

baked triple-veggie dip

PREP: 15 min. | TOTAL: 50 min. | MAKES: 4½ cups or 36 servings, 2 Tbsp. each.

▸ what you need!

1½ cups KRAFT Grated Parmesan Cheese, divided

1 can (1 lb. 3 oz.) asparagus spears, drained, chopped

1 pkg. (10 oz.) frozen chopped spinach, thawed, drained

1 can (8½ oz.) artichoke hearts, drained, chopped

1 container (8 oz.) PHILADELPHIA Chive & Onion Cream Cheese Spread

½ cup KRAFT Real Mayo Mayonnaise

▸ make it!

HEAT oven to 375°F.

MIX 1¼ cups Parmesan with all remaining ingredients.

SPOON into 2-qt. baking dish; top with remaining Parmesan.

BAKE 35 min. or until dip is heated through and top is lightly browned.

VARIATION:
Prepare as directed, using KRAFT Reduced Fat Parmesan Style Grated Topping, PHILADELPHIA Chive & Onion ⅓ Less Fat than Cream Cheese and KRAFT Mayo with Olive Oil Reduced Fat Mayonnaise.

NUTRITION BONUS:
The spinach is a good source of vitamin A in this tasty baked dip.